MPSON TECHNICAL INSTITUTE

STA
DEPT.

S0-BHX-883

LIBRARIES

MILTON

¶ JOHN MILTON was born in 1608 in Bread Street, Cheapside, in the City of London. He died in 1674 and was buried at St Giles', Cripplegate, beside his father.

MILTON

Aged twenty-one: from a copy by BENJAMIN VANDERGUCHT
(after CORNELIUS JOHNSON*) in the collection of Lord Harcourt,
and reproduced by his kind permission*

PR
3588
T6
1972

MILTON

by

E. M. W. TILLYARD

PUBLISHED FOR
THE BRITISH COUNCIL
BY LONGMAN GROUP LTD

10/10/78

14542

LONGMAN GROUP LTD
Longman House, Burnt Mill, Harlow, Essex

*Associated companies, branches and
representatives throughout the world*

First published 1952
Revised 1959
Reprinted, with additions to Bibliography, 1962, 1964, 1968, 1972
© E. M. W. Tillyard, 1959, 1972

*Printed in Great Britain by
F. Mildner & Sons, London, EC1R 5EJ*

SBN 0 582 01026 8

MILTON

I

IN *Paradise Lost* Milton described his Adam as formed for 'contemplation and valour'. He could thereby have been describing both his own nature and his own ideals. Milton was a natural Platonist, a natural seeker after perfection by high contemplation, but he also believed with Sidney that the 'ending end of all earthly learning' was 'virtuous action'. Living long before Rousseau and the age when men dreamed of human perfectibility, he believed that in this world action would always fall short of the high aims to which contemplation pointed and he would have followed Sidney once more in maintaining that 'our erected wit maketh us know what perfection is, and yet our infected will keepeth us from reaching unto it'. Nevertheless Milton's nature both craved forms of action that would not be quite unworthy of their moving principles and was sanguine enough to make him think that a great betterment of earthly conditions was possible in spite of the entrance of sin into the world. That he could combine and harmonize the elements of contemplation and of action in himself and in his poetry is one of his chief claims to greatness. But his high hopes of approximating action to ideals and of living to see a better England than the one he was born in exposed him more nakedly to the cruelty of fate than someone more sceptical and pessimistic. His final greatness consists both in the primary wealth and vitality of his nature and in the way he adjusted himself to the worst that fate could bring him.

Gifted with that ultimate simplicity of mind which Thucydides in his history and Mencius in his aphorisms called the mark of the truly great man, desiring to see life in strong clear outline, more attracted by the gold pieces than by the small change of thought, Milton was unlucky in the period of history that his life covered. It was an age of transition, belonging neither to the Renaissance confidence

that went before nor the Augustan confidence that came
after, an age in England of political division, philosophical
scepticism, and of a literature ingenious, ornate, and sophis-
ticated rather than strong and simple. Milton was very
close to his age; and the more scholars discover about him
the more sensitive they find him to the currents of contemporary thought. Yet behind this sensitiveness we can detect
the impression of Milton's not being spiritually attuned to
his setting. Fundamentally he was a Christian humanist,
a kind of rearguard of the great Renaissance army, pro-
longing the Renaissance faith in man into a less noble age, as
Hardy, though bred in an England by then predominantly
industrial, succeeded in using the relics of an older rural
England for the material of his novels.

But if Milton's life-span turned out thus unfortunate, it
was long before it definitively revealed itself to be so.
Looking back we may remark that he was born three years
after the ominous Gunpowder Plot of 1605, that the ill-
starred Charles I came to the throne at the time Milton
entered college, and that Milton's early manhood coincided
with the gradual split of the active elements of the nation
into two hostile parties. But in thus looking back and
knowing what these various happenings actually led up to
we are in a different position from Milton, who was no more
aware of the approach of civil war and all its accompanying
ills than an Englishman born in 1885 was aware of the
coming outbreak of war in 1914. To those living in
them the years in England before 1639 and 1914 seemed
good years and full of hope for better things to come.
And most of Milton's poems from before the civil war
breathe not only the vitality of youth but contentment with
the England he inhabits. In no poems more than 'L'Allegro'
and 'Il Penseroso' does this contentment show itself. He
wrote them probably near the end of his college career at
Cambridge, when he was an important figure there, and in
them he describes the joys first of the cheerful then of the
thoughtful man. And the England that provides these joys

is still the united England of the days of Elizabeth, the England that, in the words of Shakespeare, was 'true to herself':

> Som times with secure delight
> The up-land Hamlets will invite,
> When the merry Bells ring round,
> And the jocond rebecks sound
> To many a youth, and many a maid,
> Dancing in the Chequer'd shade;
> And young and old com forth to play
> On a Sunshine Holyday.
>
> ('L'Allegro', 91-8)

Nor does the young Anglican Puritan yet see anything wrong in the artistic and musical adornments of the church service:

> But let my due feet never fail
> To walk the studious Cloysters pale,
> And love the high embowed Roof,
> With antick Pillars massy proof,
> And storied Windows richly dight,
> Casting a dimm religious light.
> There let the pealing Organ blow
> To the full voic'd Quire below,
> In Service high, and Anthems cleer,
> As may with sweetnes, through mine ear,
> Dissolve me into extasies,
> And bring all Heav'n before mine eyes.
>
> ('Il Penseroso', 155-66)

A little later, in 'Arcades' and *Comus*, Milton seems to have enjoyed writing the words for that costly and aristocratic entertainment of mixed poetry, music, dancing, and scenic ingenuity, called the *masque*. This is how he turns his delicate lyric vein to compliment the grand old lady, the Countess Dowager of Derby, ancestress of many grand-children, in whose honour 'Arcades' was performed:

> Mark what radiant state she spreds,
> In circle round her shining throne,
> Shooting her beams like silver threds,

This this is she alone,
    Sitting like a Goddes bright,
    In the center of her light.

Might she the wise *Latona* be,
Or the towred *Cybele*,
Mother of a hunderd gods;
Juno dare's not give her odds;
    Who had thought this clime had held
    A deity so unparalel'd?   (14–24)

Though a strong minority of the English nobility was on the side of Parliament against the King, the masque along with other dramatic shows came to be countenanced by the Royalists alone. Milton, the future Cromwellian, writing the words for two masques so gaily and serenely, shows that men little understood the storm that threatened.

Comus, by far the longer of the two masques and the longest of Milton's early poems, reveals not only the still persisting harmony of contemporary England but the two poles of Milton's own nature, the contemplative and the active. The Attendant Spirit first pictures the earth from without, from the point of view only to be reached through meditation, talking of

    the smoak and stirr of this dim spot
Which men call Earth, and with low-thoughted care
Confin'd, and pester'd in this pin-fold here,
Strive to keep up a frail, and Feaverish being
Unmindfull of the crown that Vertue gives
After this mortal change, to her true Servants
Amongst the enthron'd gods on Sainted seats.   (5–11)

But he turns into an active character and rescues the benighted children from their danger. The Lady at her first entrance varies her speech from pure, active drama:

This way the noise was, if mine ear be true,
My best guide now, me thought it was the sound
Of Riot and ill manag'd Merriment—   (170–2)

through the shudders of romantic superstitions:

> What might this be? A thousand fantasies
> Begin to throng into my memory
> Of calling shapes, and beckning shadows dire,
> And airy tongues, that syllable mens names
> On Sands, and Shoars, and desert Wildernesses   (205-9)

to the contemplative rapture of:

> O welcom pure-ey'd Faith, white-handed Hope
> Thou hovering Angel girt with golden wings,
> And thou unblemish't form of Chastity,
> I see ye visibly.   (213-16)

Comus may not succeed completely as a whole but it shows Milton free to indulge the wealth of his nature and full of the promise of great things. Indeed in many details he has attained greatness. The second passage quoted from the Lady's speech is a poem in its own right, legitimately anthologized by Robert Bridges in *The Spirit of Man*. Only a major poet could have thought of using 'syllable' as a verb in this context. 'Syllable' is very effective onomatopœia but, through its rarity or even uniqueness in its verbal use, it also startles and makes a climax that gives the whole passage a convincing shape.

'Lycidas', published in 1637, is a rhymed poem lamenting the death of a college friend by drowning, in the strict tradition of the pastoral elegy of Greece and Rome. In it Milton at once achieved poetry of the highest order and expressed an incidental foreboding of the bitter times that were to come. There are the same large elements as in *Comus*. The element of rapturous contemplation, expressed in Lycidas's apotheosis, is there just as surely and more intensely:

> So *Lycidas* sunk low, but mounted high,
> Through the dear might of him that walk'd the waves,
> Where other groves, and other streams along,
> With *Nectar* pure his oozy Locks he laves,
> And hears the unexpressive nuptiall Song,
> In the blest Kingdoms meek of joy and love.   (172-7)

Then Milton indulges his vein of romantic description with the utmost brilliance in his imaginings of where the body of his drowned friend may have drifted:

> Whilst thee the shores, and sounding Seas
> Wash far away, where ere thy bones are hurld,
> Whether beyond the stormy *Hebrides*,
> Where thou perhaps under the whelming tide
> Visit'st the bottom of the monstrous world;
> Or whether thou to our moist vows deny'd
> Sleep'st by the fable of *Bellerus* old,
> Where the great vision of the guarded Mount
> Looks toward *Namancos* and *Bayona's* hold.　　(154–62)

And the urge to action, the will to match ideals with deeds, comes out with all the force of Milton's now mature power in the description of fame and its precariousness in this world:

> *Fame* is the spur that the clear spirit doth raise
> (That last infirmity of Noble mind)
> To scorn delights, and live laborious dayes;
> But the fair Guerdon when we hope to find,
> And think to burst out into sudden blaze,
> Comes the blind *Fury* with th' abhorred shears,
> And slits the thin spun life.　　(70–6)

But there is another side to 'Lycidas', not found in *Comus*: the political. And this side is the more important because it comes out not only in direct manner through St Peter's attack on the degenerate clergy of the day and his grim reference to the inroads of the Roman church:

> Besides what the grim Woolf with privy paw
> Daily devours apace, and nothing sed—　　(128–9)

but through a mere hint in another context: proof that Milton's mind was running on politics at this time. The two resounding lines from the end of the passage quoted about the drifting of Lycidas's body, sometimes cited to prove Milton's love of the mere sound of grandiose names, are actually packed with meaning, political included. The 'guarded Mount' is the rock-fortress of St Michael's Mount in Cornwall and the 'great vision' is the archangel himself, so called because he appeared in this place in a vision to some fishermen. Namancos and Bayona, un-identified for many years after Milton's death, are in Galicia, the Spanish Land's End. Michael, the chief warrior-angel in heaven, is on duty on his own mount near the English Land's End fixing his defensive gaze on the Spanish Land's End, to prevent both a recurrence of a Spanish Armada and the spread through Continental influence of Popery in England, of which the Puritan wing of the English Church thought there was danger through the High Church doc-trines of Laud, now at the height of his power as Arch-bishop of Canterbury.

Milton, then, in 'Lycidas' hints at the troubles to come but is far from believing them inevitable. These enrich rather than overshadow the poem. They are, indeed, an important item in the matters which burdened Milton's mind at that time and which made him wonder whether his hopes for the future were justified. But they are subordinate to the poem's great theme, the theme which coexists with the elegiac theme and of which the elegiac theme is the symbol. Milton saw that action in this world is precarious, that the good die young, that great preparations for high and vir-tuous deeds often miscarry, that the wicked often prosper. It was a painful vision, but he faced it and overcame it by the hard-won admission that results in this world do not matter and that what does matter is the state of mind behind the attempt, whether successful or not, to achieve results. Lycidas died young and achieved little; yet his state of mind was one of integrity, and his 'mounting high' into heaven symbolizes the ultimate victory of that state over what he failed to achieve by earthly action. Such was the mental conflict and the victory Milton achieved in 'Lycidas'. He was destined to fight the same fight more than once in his life—and it is a fight that cannot be avoided by anyone

who believes in the necessity at once of contemplation and of
action—but having won it on the first occasion he was not
likely to be defeated thereafter.

II

Shortly after writing 'Lycidas' (and the last line of the
poem 'To-morrow to fresh woods, and pastures new' may
refer to it) Milton set out to complete his education in the
Renaissance manner through the Grand Tour. His journey
was a happy interlude between the anxieties revealed in
'Lycidas' and the imminent civil war, and its circumstances
help us to understand Milton himself. He had no liking for
France and did not linger there, while his anxiety about
political events at home prevented him from carrying out his
plan to visit Greece. Thus his Grand Tour pretty well
resolved itself into a long residence in different parts of Italy.
There is every indication that Milton adored Italy and that
he was a great success there. Certainly the actual country
left its mark on his later poetry. Here, for instance, is a
reference to a scene in Tuscany: in the first book of *Paradise
Lost*, Satan, having painfully reached the beach of the fiery
lake where he had lain prone:

> stood and calld
> His Legions, Angel Forms, who lay intranst
> Thick as Autumnal Leaves that strow the Brooks
> In *Vallombrosa*, where th' *Etrurian* shades
> High overarch't imbowr.   (300–4)

It has been argued very plausibly that the landscape of
Milton's Hell derives its details from the volcanic region near
Naples known as the Phlegraean Fields, while I have little
doubt, though I have not met the notion elsewhere, that the
garden of the Villa d'Este at Tivoli with its abundance of
water drawn from the Anio, its slopes and terraces, and its
luxuriance was at the back of Milton's mind when he created
his Paradise. But there were more things than the land-

scape to attract Milton to Italy. By the year 1638, when Milton reached Italy, the cultural centre of Europe had shifted thence to France; and Italy was living on its past rather than facing the future. The spirit of the Renaissance, prevalent so much earlier in Italy than in the rest of western Europe, lingered there the longest; and it was here above all that Milton could find an intellectual temper really to his taste. Not that we should make Milton's success in Italy a small matter or underestimate his remarkable powers of self-adaptation to a foreign setting. It speaks very highly indeed for the flexibility and richness of his temperament that he, bred in a Puritan family and in the more Puritan of the two Universities, strongly opposed politically to the Roman Church and to any romanizing tendencies in his own, and professing an austere morality, should have grown so much at home in the centre of Catholicism and in a land where morals were far from austere. And he did so at no sacrifice whatever of his own private standards.

Coming back to England in 1639, Milton was caught in the uprush of enthusiasm that carried away the Parliamentary party and the reforming wing of the English Church. There was the chance, he believed, that food might after all be provided for the 'hungry sheep' of England, who, he had complained in 'Lycidas', 'looked up' and were 'not fed'. So believing, he could not hold back. 'Virtuous action' for him now lay in the region of politics and not of poetry where he had wanted it to be. When Milton committed himself he did so with all his heart and he devoted himself to politics instead of poetry for many years to come. And his return to poetry was along the sad road of political disillusionment.

But at first his hopes ran high. He believed with other sincere and ardent men that if the English Church could be further reformed, if in particular the Episcopacy could be abolished, a new golden age would be established in England; and he pictured himself as the poet chosen to celebrate the new order:

Then, amidst the hymns and hallelujahs of saints, some one may perhaps be heard offering at high strains in new and lofty measures to sing and celebrate thy divine mercies and marvellous judgments in this land throughout all ages; whereby this great and warlike nation, instructed and inured to the fervent and continual practice of truth and righteousness, and casting far from her the rags of her old vices, may press on hard to that high and happy emulation to be found the soberest, wisest, and most Christian people.

This is superbly said but it shows the weakness of Milton as politician. Such fervour befits ideals but not Acts of Parliament. And when the Presbyterian superseded the Episcopal form of Church government in England Milton was forced to admit that the change did not bring in the millennium and that 'new Presbyter was but old Priest writ large'. Under the Commonwealth Milton worked for what we now call the Foreign Office and, after the precedent of Chaucer and Spenser, was an efficient government servant; but he was too much of an idealist to be able to hedge and compromise over the large issues that concern the high politician and that have to be reduced from their Utopian potentialities to the scanty proportions of what will work in the shabby, mean-principled world of every day. Milton's pamphlets, his major expression of high political opinion, are not successful as practical tracts for the times. When he is exalted he is too remote from the real world; when he forces himself to be controversial and lowers his tone he carries abuse too far to be effective. Nevertheless, considered not as effective political writing but as independent prose works, Milton's pamphlets, uneven as they are, form a wonderful body of vivid and varied and powerful prose, illustrating like his earlier poetry his belief in both contemplation and action, and presenting certain sides of his character that might not, though surely there, have been detected in his verse.

I need not dwell on the theme of action in Milton's prose, for most of it is in itself a form of action, and efforts to persuade men to follow this or that course. What is to the

point is to show how Milton's belief in contemplation keeps
breaking out in contexts that should be severely practical.
Thus, in one of his pamphlets against the Bishops, *The Reason
of Church-Government urg'd against Prelaty* (1641-2), he
inserts a long personal passage in which he talks of his
poetic plans and of his conception of the poet's high office.
A true poem, he holds, is

> not to be raised from the heat of youth, or the vapours of wine, like that
> which flows at waste from the pen of some vulgar amorist or the trencher
> fury of a rhyming parasite; nor to be obtained by the invocation of dame
> memory and her siren daughters, but by devout prayer to that eternal
> Spirit, who can enrich with all utterance and knowledge and sends out his
> Seraphim with the hallowed fire of his altar to touch and purify the lips
> of whom he pleases.

And if the eternal Spirit is ready to inspire, he will inspire
the man who has by the act of contemplation prepared his
heart for the inspiration, for Milton goes on to talk of
'beholding the bright countenance of truth in the quiet and
still air of delightful studies'. Milton is here remote indeed
from the grasping and opportunist world of political action.

What are the sides of Milton's nature that his prose makes
especially clear, and which readers might overlook in his
verse?

First, the man's uncommon exuberance. Milton's total
poetic output is not large, and we might be tempted to think
that he wrote slowly and painfully. If we heed the torrent
of his prose with its immensely wealthy vocabulary, we can
be sure that Milton wrote comparatively little poetry only
because he rejected so much and selected so fastidiously. By
nature he had the exuberance of a Rubens, but it was
checked and compressed by the severity and the scrupulous-
ness of a Racine. But in prose Milton felt no obligation to
curb his magnanimity or to comb out his vocabulary. He
bursts out into vivid metaphors and allows his sentences to
grow to great lengths through sheer sustention of vitality.
Here, for instance, is his invective, from his tract *Of Education*
(1644), against the system of studies still prevalent at the

λ 0009253

Universities with its disastrous effect on the undergraduates' future careers:

And for the usual method of teaching arts, I deem it to be an old error of universities, not yet well recovered from the scholastic grossness of barbarous ages, that instead of beginning with arts most easy (and those be such as are most obvious to the sense) they present their young unmatriculated novices at first coming with the most intellective abstractions of logic and metaphysics, so that they having but newly left those grammatic flats and shallows, where they stuck unreasonably to learn a few words with lamentable construction, and now on a sudden transported under another climate to be tossed and turmoiled with their unballasted wits in fathomless and unquiet deeps of controversy, do for the most part grow into hatred and contempt of learning, mocked and deluded all this while with ragged notions and babblements while they expected worthy and delightful knowledge, till poverty or youthful years call them importunately their several ways and hasten them with the sway of friends either to an ambitious and mercenary or ignorantly zealous divinity: some allured to the trade of law, grounding their purposes not on the prudent and heavenly contemplation of justice and equity, which was never taught them, but on the promising and pleasing thoughts of litigious terms, fat contentions, and flowing fees; others betake them to state affairs with souls so unprincipled in virtue and true generous breeding that flattery and court-shifts and tyrannous aphorisms appear to them the highest points of wisdom, instilling their barren hearts with a conscientious slavery; others, lastly, of a more delicious and airy spirit retire themselves to the enjoyments of ease and luxury, living out their days in feast and jollity, which indeed is the wisest and safest course of all these unless they were with more integrity undertaken—and these are the fruits of misspending our prime youth at the schools and universities as we do, either in learning mere words or such things chiefly as were better unlearned.

This is at once a single sentence and a whole paragraph. Milton's ardour presses on unremitting to the end.

Secondly, there appears in Milton's prose, fitfully it is true, a sense of humour. This comes out, naturally, at odd moments and in chance phrases, at times when his feelings have cooled and he is not concerned with a main argument. At the end of *Colasterion* (1645), a hot piece of controversy on the subject of divorce, Milton says how glad he is to have done with his adversary:

At any hand I would be rid of him; for I had rather, since the life of man is likened to a scene, that all my entrances and exits might mix with such persons only whose worth erects them and their actions to a grave and tragic deportment and not to have to do with clowns and vices. But if a man cannot peaceably walk into the world but must be infested, sometimes at his face with dorrs and horseflies, sometimes beneath with bawling whippets and shin-barkers . . . have I not cause to be in such a manner defensive as may procure me freedom to pass unmolested hereafter?

The general tone is scornful, but no man without a sense of humour could have coined the phrase *bawling whippets and shin-barkers*. In *Areopagitica* (1644), the most lively and varied and readable of all the pamphlets, there occurs a delightfully humorous description of the wealthy merchant who finds 'religion to be a traffic so entangled . . . that he cannot skill to keep a stock going upon that trade' and who solves his problem by hiring a tame clergyman to deputize, 'resigning the whole warehouse of his religion, with all the locks and keys, into his custody'.

If the prose tells us certain things about Milton, so do his sonnets, written like the prose mostly between 'Lycidas' and *Paradise Lost*. Like some of Horace's *Odes* (on which they are partly modelled) and many of Hardy's lyrics, they are occasional poems dealing with people or contemporary events. That Milton should write sonnets to Fairfax, Cromwell, and other Parliamentary leaders is not surprising and accords with his prose. What most adds to our knowledge of the man are the feelings he displays in the personal sonnets: his tenderness towards his second wife, now dead; his uncomplaining humility in the sonnet on his blindness; the urbanity with which in the following he invites his friend Lawrence to dinner:

> *Lawrence*, of vertuous Father vertuous Son,
>   Now that the Fields are dank, and ways are mire,

> Where shall we sometimes meet, and by the fire
> Help waste a sullen day; what may be won
> From the hard Season gaining: time will run
> On smoother, till *Favonius* re-inspire
> The frozen earth; and cloath in fresh attire
> The Lillie and Rose, that neither sow'd nor spun.
> What neat repast shall feast us, light and choice,
> Of Attick tast, with Wine, whence we may rise
> To hear the Lute well toucht, or artfull voice
> Warble immortal Notes and *Tuskan* Ayre?
> He who of those delights can judge, and spare
> To interpose them oft, is not unwise.   (xx)

I have written thus far of the pamphlets and the sonnets as isolated works, possessing certain literary qualities and telling us things about Milton's nature. They also, when taken in sequence, tell the story of how his hopes of national betterment through high action came to grief, and of his own personal disasters or disappointments. Milton did not abandon his hopes lightly. It is true that the defeat of the episcopacy and the victory of presbyterianism did not produce the wonderful betterment he expected. But presbyterianism had not come to stay, and better things might issue from the professions of greater religious toleration put out by the Independents. Moreover the very richness and fervour of religious controversy gave Milton grounds for hope. *Areopagitica*, written after the first decisive victory of the Parliament at Marston Moor and when there was the promise of opposition to the now established Presbyterians, utters this hope. This pamphlet, the classic plea in literature for liberty of the Press, is also an utterance of hope that England is about to enter a new era of free vitality, when, unrestricted by the harsh decrees of ecclesiastical orthodoxy, she may both face the full truth of God's word and be strong and virtuous enough to draw sustenance and life from it:

Methinks I see in my mind a noble and puissant nation rousing herself like a strong man after sleep and shaking her invincible locks: methinks I see her as an eagle mewing her mighty youth and kindling her undazzled eyes at the full midday beam, purging and scaling her long-abused sight at the fountain itself of heavenly radiance.

Note once again in this passage the union of action and contemplation: the references first to Samson with his uncut hair, the man of great deeds, and then to the eagle symbolizing in its supposed power to envisage the sun the mind that has the strength to contemplate the Platonic ideas or God himself.

The story of Milton's disillusion is the story of England between *Areopagitica*, written in 1644, and the Restoration in 1660. Parliament won the war but failed to win the hearts of the English people. Representing at first a majority of the population, the Parliamentary rulers became themselves fewer and represented an ever dwindling minority. Of that minority Milton was an absolutely loyal member, his own high idealism drawing him to those who for whatever reason were willing to go to extremes. Here at least, he felt, were real men and not time-servers or Laodiceans; and in some of his sonnets and in his great Latin prose work, *The Second Defence of the English People*, he celebrated their virtues and gave them high advice. But all the time he knew that these heroic men had not got the country behind them, and he experienced a great revulsion from the sentiments about it expressed in the passage quoted from *Areopagitica*. He thinks now that lethargy is the besetting vice of most of his countrymen. It was lethargy, he thought, that caused them to sympathize with Charles for all his misdeeds and to withdraw their support from the men who had dared to put him to death; for lethargy cannot bear change, however called for, and the desire for a king was of long and rooted growth. Not that Milton despaired when men regretted Charles; on the contrary he vented his hopes and his energies in writing in support of the regicides. His vehement efforts were the final reason for his loss of sight. But he never regretted the sacrifice, as he told Cyriack Skinner in a sonnet; nor does he argue

> Against heavns hand or will, nor bate a jot
> Of heart or hope; but still bear up and steer
> Right onward.   (xxii)

This is indeed to apply the lesson of 'Lycidas', the lesson that
the deed's motive, not its result, matters.

III

Milton's blindness had the effect of detaching him
gradually from his position as government servant. Through
his Latin defences of the regicides he earned the government's gratitude at home and fame abroad; but as a blind
man he could no longer be of the same use. Released from
regular employment, though still good for an occasional
pamphlet, he returned to his plans for a great poem some
four years before the Restoration.

His other personal trouble was the unhappy beginning of
his first marriage. His wife returned to her parents probably
a little more than a year after the wedding. But we must
remember that she returned to him and bore him children,
and that his two other marriages were happy. With little
knowledge of the feminine heart before marriage he acquired
a sufficiency by the time he came to write *Paradise Lost*.

With Cromwell's death and the plain imminence of the
restoration of the Stuarts Milton still refused to give up hope
but risked his life by writing last-minute appeals to the
English people not to submit their necks to a tyrant. The
actual shock of the Restoration must have been terrible.
There is no record of his feelings unless, as has been conjec-
tured, he composed *Samson Agonistes* while in hiding and
in danger of execution. But if Samson's dejection reflects,
as it may well do, feelings which Milton at one time
experienced, it may plausibly concern the loss of sight that
was common to them both. We shall be safer if we recon-
struct Milton's feelings at the time of the Restoration from
his more firmly dated works. However great the shock of

the Restoration (and its magnitude must have corresponded roughly with the vehemence of Milton's pamphleteering immediately before it) I believe he must have faced beforehand the failure of his hopes, just as a good commander will have faced the problem of extricating his troops, should the victory he so passionately desires be denied him. And the evidence is the general scheme of *Paradise Lost*, begun, and hence we may be certain in the case of so rigorously architectonic a poet as Milton already planned, some four years before the Restoration. The general scheme of *Paradise Lost* embodies the moral of 'Lycidas': that results matter less than states of mind. Satan's apparently decisive act in causing man's fall, an act based on an envious and cruel state of mind, ends by being less strong than the small sound human acts of mutual generosity and of repentance performed by Adam and Eve after they have fallen. If Milton had staked everything on the results of his political hopes he could never have framed his poem in this way. That he cared greatly about the Restoration is proved by his pamphlets, that he had also learnt not to care is proved by the scheme of *Paradise Lost*. That it cost him dear to learn not to care, and that he did suffer mental torment when his hopes failed we cannot doubt.

Milton planned to make a single great poem the crown of his life, to do for his own country what Homer, Virgil, Camões, and Tasso had done for theirs. I believe that in *Paradise Lost* he succeeded and hence I have intended my remarks so far to lead up to this poem. All the qualities so far enumerated find a place there. As I shall point out in detail it largely concerns action and the proper grounds for it. The side of contemplation is included partly through the many shifts of distance from which action is viewed, partly through descriptions which suggest a static condition of eternity rather than the shifting phenomena of this world. The pageants of earthly history Michael shows to Adam are seen as if from a distance, and Adam's comment on them at the end fixes this impression:

> How soon hath thy prediction, Seer blest,
> Measur'd this transient World, the Race of time,
> Till time stand fixt: beyond is all abyss,
> Eternitie, whose end no eye can reach.   (XII. 553–6)

The account of Paradise, though in the first instance
borrowed from an actual garden, ends by speaking of an
imagined world of incredible static beauty and felicity.
Politics, though subordinated to a moral theme that goes far
beyond them, are included through the infernal debates in
the second book and through the characters of the different
speakers. I shall refer later to instances of humour and
generally to the diversity of the poem, to Milton's success in
including in its compass all experience as he knew it.

Up to *Paradise Lost* the facts of Milton's life sometimes
help us to understand his writing; and *Paradise Lost* itself is
clearer if we know the conditions that led up to it. But
after 1660 Milton lived anything but a public life, and there
is little profit in connecting poetry and biography. Thus,
from now on I am concerned with his poetry alone.

The fall of man was not Milton's first choice for the subject of his great poem. At the time of his Italian journey he
intended to write on King Arthur, and there are passages in
his earliest pamphlets that show the kind of poem it would
have been. It would have been partly religious and moral,
partly patriotic. Arthur would have borne something of
the character of Spenser's Prince Arthur in the *Faerie Queene*,
uniting the contemplative and active virtues but unlike
Spenser's he would have been the centre of action in defeat-
ing the heathen Saxon invaders. British history, again as in
Spenser, would have been narrated in prophecy culminating
in the defeat of the Spanish Armada. The main emphasis
would have been on heroic action. If there had been no
civil war and Milton had been free to write his Arthuriad
around the time of *Areopagitica* he would have given us a
divinely energetic poem but less varied and less mature than
Paradise Lost. He might have gone on to a second, more

mature poem; and the two together might have had an even wider scope than *Paradise Lost*. But if the choice were between an Arthuriad and *Paradise Lost*, we should be content with what we have.

Milton's very earliest critics served him well. Sir Henry Wotton, commenting on *Comus* in 1638, spoke of 'a certain Dorique delicacy in your Songs and Odes, whereunto I must plainly confess to have seen yet nothing parallel in our Language'. Wotton was thinking of all the parts of *Comus* not in dramatic blank verse, but 'Doric delicacy' describes like no other phrase the mixture of austerity and sensuous sweetness that generally marks Milton's early poetry. Andrew Marvell supplied a set of commendatory verses to the second edition of *Paradise Lost* which show a just appreciation of the poem's scope and versification. He described the scope of Milton's subject thus:

> *Messiah* Crown'd, Gods Reconcil'd Decree,
> Rebelling Angels, the Forbidden Tree,
> Heav'n, Hell, Earth, Chaos, All:

showing that he saw that the actual loss of Paradise was but a fraction of the whole. And this is his account of Milton's style:

> At once delight and horrour on us seise,
> Thou singst with so much gravity and ease;
> And above humane flight dost soar aloft
> With Plume so strong, so equal, and so soft.

'Softness and ease': these are the qualities of style in *Paradise Lost* often unrecognized by those who are too intent on his gravity and sublimity. Dryden, who praises *Paradise Lost* unstintingly, is yet the first critic to interpret it wrongly. He said in 1697 that Milton would have a better claim to have written a genuine epic, 'if the Devil had not been his hero instead of Adam, if the giant had not foiled the knight and driven him out of his stronghold to wander through the world with his lady errant'. There you have that undue

narrowing of the poem's scope to the episode of the Fall and
the triumph of Satan: a narrowing that has become traditional and still continues to close the eyes of many readers
and critics to the poem's full significance. It is true that
Milton himself gave countenance to this narrowing by the
title he gave his epic, though I sometimes think that he was
being ironical and meant us to think of *Lost* as in inverted
commas. But Dryden's witty contention that the giant
foiled the knight is quite at odds with the poem itself.

Paradise Lost in its grand outlines is founded on a simple
irony. And we need not be surprised, for irony is one of
the qualities Milton gives to God the Father himself.
When near the beginning of the third book the Father looks
down and sees Satan 'coasting the wall of Heav'n' and about
to penetrate the universe, he addresses the Son as follows:

> Onely begott'n Son, seest thou what rage
> Transports our adversarie, whom no bounds
> Prescrib'd, no barrs of Hell, nor all the chains
> Heapt on him there, nor yet the main Abyss
> Wide interrupt can hold?   (III. 80-4)

One critic accused Milton here of inconsistency because
when in the first book Satan raised himself from the burning
lake Milton tells us he did so only through the 'will and
high permission of all-ruling Heaven'. Of course there is
no inconsistency, for in the passage quoted the Father
speaks ironically, adopting Satan's own foolish assumption
that he raised himself from the lake and set out to ruin mankind on his own initiative and responsibility alone. If we
grasp God's ironical words at Satan's expense we may be the
readier to believe that irony is central to the whole plot.
The irony is as follows. Satan succeeds in tempting mankind to transgress God's commandment and he believes that
his success can have only one result: as Satan and his fellows
have brought complete ruin on themselves by disobedience,
so must Adam and Eve do by theirs. But he has made a
false comparison. Satan's sin was self-motivated, that of

Adam and Eve was partly motivated from without. For
Satan there is no hope, for he is corrupt throughout his
whole being; for Adam and Eve there is hope, because
theirs was not the whole responsibility. And in the end
humanity finds itself able to attain an inner paradise better
than the paradise they must give up; Dryden's knight and
lady errant have in fact the key to a better stronghold than
the one from which the giant has driven them out. Such
is the irony at Satan's expense. There is the further irony
that Adam and Eve are as mistaken as Satan about their
ultimate fate. When, exhausted by their quarrels and
bereft of their pride, they become reconciled in very simple
human companionship and fellow-feeling, they are quite
unaware that they are following the promptings both of
heaven and of the residue of good thoughts that have sur-
vived the Fall and that by so following they have attained
salvation: just as the Ancient Mariner blessed the water-
snakes unawares, not knowing that thereby he had broken
the evil spell.

There are important consequences of this fundamental
irony. First, the weight of the plot is put not on the mere
episode of Eve eating the apple in the ninth book but on the
whole process of temptation, Fall, the judgement by the Son
of the Serpent, Adam and Eve; on the corruption of the
world through the entry of Sin and the consequent despair
of Adam and Eve; and then, unexpectedly evolved out of all
these varied and vast happenings, their mutual reconcilia-
tion, their penitence before God, and their salvation. These
happenings occupy the whole of Books IX and X.
Such a weighting of the plot is of the first moment. The
fall of Eve, adequate enough in a larger ironic context, is
nowhere near weighty enough, as described by Milton, to be
the centre of the poem, the point to which all earlier
happenings lead and from which all subsequent happenings
derive. But read Books IX and X as a unit, treat the
events after the Fall not as appendices to a completed climax
but as a sequence leading up to the real climax in man's

regeneration, and you find them a brilliantly diversified and massive area of high poetry, a principal glory of the English tongue. It may be asked whether the climax as thus described will really bear the weight put on it any more than the traditionally assumed climax, the eating of the apple. Can this purely human scene of man and wife forgetting their quarrels, coming together again, and confessing their sin to God stand the tremendous test? First, it can be retorted that Milton undoubtedly intended it to do so. Near the end of the whole poem there is a conversation between Adam and Michael which follows on the vision of future world history Michael has given to Adam for his instruction. From its all-important position and its intensely concentrated and earnest tone it is clearly crucial to the poem's meaning. Adam has at last learnt wisdom, and this is his statement of some of the things hard experience has taught him:

> Henceforth I learne, that to obey is best,
> And love with feare the onely God, to walk
> As in his presence, ever to observe
> His providence, and on him sole depend,
> Merciful over all his works, with good
> Still overcoming evil, and by small
> Accomplishing great things, by things deemd weak
> Subverting worldly strong, and worldly wise
> By simply meek.   (XII. 561–9)

This is high moralizing verse that would be irrelevant in a narrative poem if it did not repeat in its own abstract form what had already been transacted in concrete, dramatic action; and it points precisely to the poem's true climax where by their 'small' decent action Adam and Eve 'accomplish great things' and in their apparent 'weakness subvert' the apparently 'strong' machinations of the prince of this world. Whether Milton not only intended to make this part of the poem his climax but succeeded in making it a worthy one can only be decided by the verdict

of competent readers; but to me at least the account of
Adam's black despair, his ferocious and cruel repulse of Eve,
her persistence, Adam's softening towards her, their coming
together, Eve's still distraught state of mind and inclination
to suicide, Adam's strong and comforting words, and their
final resolution to confess their sins to God is true to the
fundamental simplicities of human nature and composes one
of the most moving dramatic episodes in literature; it can
bear a very heavy weight.

The second consequence of recognizing the poem's
fundamental irony is that it puts Satan in his proper place.
Dryden has had many distinguished successors in his heresy
that Satan is the hero; and as long as Adam and Eve were
denied heroic action in their recovery after the Fall it was
indeed natural to fill the resulting vacuum with any other
action that had heroic pretensions. And that action was the
escape of Satan from the fiery lake in Hell, and his courage
in undertaking alone the journey to Earth for the ruin of
mankind. But Milton's Satan is never a hero, he is an
archangel ruined: that terrible thing—a being with great
potentialities of good corrupted; graced indeed, to heighten
the drama, with some relics of good feelings but doomed to
turn those relics to even greater evil. Those who have
sentimentalized Satan have failed to see the coarseness and
the vulgarity that accompany and darken these lingering
relics of good feeling. Here is Milton's description of
Satan reviewing the army of devils now mustered in Hell:

> Hee through the armed Files
> Darts his experienc't eye, and soon traverse
> The whole Battalion views; thir order due,
> Thir visages and stature as of Gods;
> Thir number last he summs. And now his heart
> Distends with pride, and hardning in his strength
> Glories.   (I. 567–73)

It is a most damning description. How significant the
juxtaposition of number and pride. Satan is revealed

as the vulgarian who is thrilled by mere quantity. No wonder he commits a fundamental error in his estimate of what fate awaits disobedient man. All this is not to deny Satan's grandeur. It is just because he combines grandeur with vulgarity, a commanding intellect with a fundamental stupidity, not to speak of other discrepant qualities, that he is so true to life and so eternally fascinating a figure.

The fundamental irony at Satan's expense and at the apparent expense but to the ultimate profit of Adam and Eve is surpassingly powerful because it grew out of Milton's life-experience and provided the most authentic material for his supreme poetic gift; a gift both congenital and improved by intense study. Milton condemns pride with such authority because he was himself strongly tempted to it. Compare him in this matter with Shakespeare. There is in literature no finer indictment of pride than Isabella's speech to Angelo in *Measure for Measure*:

> Could great men thunder
> As Jove himself does, Jove would ne'er be quiet,
> For every pelting, petty officer
> Would use his heaven for thunder;
> Nothing but thunder . . . Merciful heaven,
> Thou rather with thy sharp and sulphurous bolt,
> Splits the unwedgeable and gnarléd oak
> Than the soft myrtle; but man, proud man,
> Drest in a little brief authority,
> Most ignorant of what he's most assured—
> His glassy essence—like an angry ape,
> Plays such fantastic tricks before high heaven
> As make the angels weep.   (II.ii. 111–23)

In his history plays, too, Shakespeare gives convincing pictures of proud and ambitious and unscrupulous men. But Isabella's speech and Shakespeare's quarrelling nobles are passionately observed, not created out of the personal stuff of Shakespeare's mind. He could objectify them from the beginning unhampered by any unusual personal involvement. But, as his pamphlets clearly show, Milton did suffer from that impatient pride which revolts against the nature of things and which demands quick results; he had an element of Satan in him; and he experienced the despairing bafflement that such pride is bound to end in. But, as 'Lycidas' showed, he was also aware of this side of his nature and hated it, believing even more passionately in the need for humility. And always the victory of humility was complete. It is because of this personal conflict, absent from Shakespeare in this acute form, that the basic irony of *Paradise Lost* has its peculiar power. Milton did objectify his material: we do not in reading *Paradise Lost* think of Milton the man. But he objectified with greater difficulty and at a later stage of the poetic process than Shakespeare did; and his poetry makes a different impression. Shakespeare was very close to life; Milton to his own life. And the Miltonic closeness has its own superb authenticity.

I have asserted that the basis of *Paradise Lost* is a great irony expressive of a great piece of simple morality, and that Milton's own total experience of this morality makes his poem authentic. We are reluctant, however, to accept a piece of simple morality as authentic unless it is supported by a big mass of detail. We require a poet to talk about many things before we are ready to accept what he most has to say. So I come now by a quite natural sequence to the various parts of *Paradise Lost*. These are so many that I will have to select; and I will do so by dealing only with those things which have either been denied to Milton or, if granted to him, ignored or slurred over or deprecated.

First, there is the theology. While the eighteenth century was too prone to see in *Paradise Lost* a simple orthodoxy, the late nineteenth and early twentieth centuries were too prone to cut out the theology altogether as an unfortunate accretion, dictated by the conditions of seventeenth-century England. The truth is that Milton's theology is not entirely orthodox and that it is inseparable from the poem. If, as I assert, the main theme of the poem has to do with pride and

humility, these qualities are not independent and uncircum-
stantiated but bear the form, inescapable in the post-classical
tradition in Europe, given them by Christianity. However
much Milton had tried to free himself from theological ties,
Pride as he presented it would in some sort have remained
the chief of the Seven Deadly Sins, and humility a quality
exemplified in the story of Christ as told in the New
Testament. When in 'Lycidas' Milton implies the doctrine of
disinterestedness he gives us neither the abstracted doctrine
nor the form of it found in the Bhagavad-Gita. However
universal the doctrine, Christian and Indian writers had to
present it in the ways they had inherited. Readers today
are better placed to accept Milton's theology because recent
scholarship has been teaching them a great deal about the
theological tradition Milton inherited. So long as readers
conceived it as a narrow fundamentalism of the kind described in the Mark Rutherford novels, they had to free
Milton the poet from it. But if they realize that for Milton,
as for his predecessors, theology included all philosophy and
a great deal of natural science, they will see that such sever-
ance is not only unnecessary but disastrously weakening
to the range of Milton's interests.

One of the great theological doctrines was that a main
way to approach God was through studying the beautiful
variety of his creation. I have already mentioned the
exuberance of Milton's nature as something fundamental.
Possessing it he was bound to find the bounty of nature both
exciting and satisfying. Living when he did and brought
up as he was, he cannot conceive of this bounty in other than
theological terms. He must see it in terms of the great
orderly arrangement of the total creation pictured as a great
hierarchical chain stretching from the Seraph nearest the
throne of God to the meanest speck of inanimate matter.
Even when Comus, the champion of disorder, speaks of the
bounty of God's creation that he may tempt the Lady to
licence he does so with an enthusiasm that can be best
matched in the panegyrics of orthodox divinity:

Wherefore did Nature powre her bounties forth,
With such a full and unwithdrawing hand,
Covering the earth with odours, fruits, and flocks,
Thronging the Seas with spawn innumerable?   (710–13)

And when in *Paradise Lost* Milton writes of free will, he
colours a doctrine that was essential to his own nature with
traditional disputes over predestination and with the special
Protestant doctrine of Christian liberty based on the writings
of St Paul. Milton's theology, far from being a tie, an
alien thing, was a great world of thought where an
immensely wide range of passions could find their natural
embodiments.

Great poets are often the subject of large popular misconceptions. Chaucer has been thought of as hearty,
Shakespeare as uneducated and unacademic, Shelley as
weakly neurotic, Milton as inhuman and humourless. And
these misconceptions die hard. It may be difficult therefore
to gain the reader's ear if one points to humour and a delicate
human perception in *Paradise Lost*. Humour, indeed, is not
what one is led to expect in the straight epic from Virgil
onward; nor could humour be advertised in the uniform
metre of the epic with the clarity possible in a play using
both verse and prose like Shakespeare's *Henry IV*. But
Milton expects his readers to be 'fit' as well as 'few'; and
'fitness' indicates close reading, which in its turn reveals,
perhaps as a great surprise, these qualities of humour and
delicate human perception. I mentioned earlier the wealthy
city merchant in *Areopagitica*, who hired a divine to manage
his religion for him, as a humorous figure; and I fancy he
reappears in a passage of *Paradise Lost* which has been pointed
to as an example of Milton's seeking to be funny with
disastrous results. It occurs just before the great description
of Paradise and it is a comparison with the way Satan over-
leaped the leafy barriers of that place, scorning entry by the
proper way:

   Or as a Thief bent to unhoord the cash

Of some rich Burgher, whose substantial dores,
Cross-barrd and bolted fast, fear no assault,
In at the window climbes, or ore the tiles.   (IV. 188–91)

The point of the whole passage is to lower the dignity of
Satan, who a little before has struck a highly dramatic
attitude, by homely comparisons, so that the reader may
have his mind cleared for the coming description of Paradise;
but the actual lines are a piece of satirical humour at the
expense of the rich merchant who is imaginative enough to
guard against direct assault but not imaginative enough to
forestall a cat-burglar.

I remarked earlier that Milton acquired a knowledge of
the other sex during the years of the Commonwealth, and in
Paradise Lost this knowledge comes, as we might expect, in
the later books where the action has converged from Hell
and Heaven on to the universe and finally on to the narrow
human stage of the mount of Paradise. It is in the long
scene near the beginning of Book IX where Adam and
Eve discuss whether they shall garden separately or jointly
that the human comedy is most evident. That Milton
dared to introduce comedy immediately before the great
disaster in human history is quite amazing; and, if that
disaster had been irreparable, comedy would have been out
of the question. But I do not see how any careful and
honest reader can miss the comedy; and I fancy Milton
introduced it because he wished to relieve the disaster of the
Fall itself of too stark an emphasis and to prepare for the
basic irony of the poem. The dispute between Adam and
Eve is as delicate a piece of domestic comedy as you could
find. Eve proposes separate gardening this particular
morning not because she really wants that but because she
wants Adam to say that he loves her too much to bear to be
separated from her. Adam falls into the trap and replies
with a heavy piece of moralizing. Eve gets her own back
by saying that Adam does not trust her. Adam grows
seriously concerned and argues earnestly, even impressively;

and, if only he could have seen it, Eve was by now quite satisfied with the effect that her stratagem had produced. But Adam does not see and refuses the responsibility of keeping Eve at his side. Finally Eve feels that after all this she cannot now refuse the offer of a freedom she did not really want at any time, and now less than ever. And so they part, and Eve is exposed alone to the wiles of Satan. It is a perfect picture of the sort of misunderstanding that can afflict any ordinary well-intentioned married couple; and it is proof that Milton had an eye for ordinary human traffic as well as for God's empyrean. Most remarkable is the stylistic skill by which he keeps the comedy from being cheap, so that it can slide into the tragic; for Adam's failure to assert himself at the right moment was not only comedy but a tragic moral lapse.

But Milton's success in passing from comedy to tragedy was possible only within a restricted area of contrast. Obliged by writing in the epic form to observe a certain kind of uniformity, he has to pitch his comedy in a higher style than was required for the drama; his conversational cadences have to blend with a modicum of pomp. The conversational cadence of Eve's reprimand to Adam:

> But that thou shouldst my firmness therfore doubt
> To God or thee, because we have a foe
> May tempt it, I expected not to hear,   (IX. 279–81)

with its stresses on *thou* and *my* is perfect, but it is delicately, not blatantly, conveyed; and the dignity of the passage does not fall below the standard expected from epic writing in the seventeenth century. It is this delicacy and lack of blatancy that both separates Milton's art from that of the Metaphysical poets and exaggerates that separation. The Metaphysicals founded their art on surprise and advertised what they were doing with much emphasis. Milton resembled them in being full of surprises but he was extremely discreet about them. Had he not been full of surprises he would have been untrue to the age in which he lived; had he paraded the fact he would have been intolerable as an epic poet.

The matter of surprise is connected with another: that of realism. Milton's epic has the remotest possible setting, yet he wished its application to be entirely modern. To achieve his end he constantly refers on passing to contemporary events or interests and slips the homely and the sensuous into contexts that are grandoise and remote. In the high description of Satan's lieutenants in Book I Milton suddenly inserts his reference to the riotous young men who made the streets of London dangerous in the later years of his life:

> And when Night
> Darkens the Streets, then wander forth the Sons
> Of *Belial*, flown with insolence and wine.

It is a startling piece of realism but slipped in so coolly and quietly that it does not impair the epic texture. In the last lines of the poem, which gave the vast picture of the angels thrusting Adam and Eve out of the gates of Paradise, occurs a reference of the greatest possible homeliness: to an ordinary peasant returning home to supper on a misty evening. I give it in its setting.

> So spake our Mother *Eve*, and *Adam* heard
> Well pleas'd, but answer'd not; for now too nigh
> Th'Archangel stood, and from the other Hill
> To thir fixt Station, all in bright array
> The Cherubim descended; on the ground
> Gliding meteorous, as Ev'ning Mist
> Ris'n from a River ore the marish glides,
> And gathers ground fast at the Labourers heel
> Homeward returning. High in Front advanc't,
> The brandisht Sword of God before them blaz'd
> Fierce as a Comet; which with torrid heat,
> And vapour as the *Libyan* Air adust,
> Began to parch that temperate Clime; whereat
> In either hand the hastning Angel caught
> Our lingring Parents and to th'Eastern Gate
> Led them direct, and down the Cliff as fast
> To the subjected Plaine; then, disappeerd.

They looking back, all th'Eastern side beheld
Of Paradise, so late thir happie seat,
Wav'd over by that flaming Brand, the Gate
With dreadful Faces throngd and fierie Armes.

(XII. 624–44)

I quoted this passage to illustrate how successfully Milton
could insinuate the homely and the realistic into the grandiose: but it will serve also to prompt a final general comment on *Paradise Lost*. It is one of the great passages and it
is typical of the poem generally in uniting so many strands
and grades of feeling: the huge almost monstrous picture of
the thronged gate and the miniature picture of the two
human beings; the Archangel matched by the peasant;
the particularity of description of the 'Eastern Gate' set
against the symbolic significance of the 'subjected Plaine'.
And these many strands are made to co-operate through
their common subordination to a unifying though never
monotonous type of verse. Such is the general nature of
Paradise Lost and it corresponds to the primary wealth and
vitality of Milton's own nature and to the mental discipline
through which he accepted and held together the good and
the ill that life brought him.

Paradise Lost is exacting because it is a long, highly concentrated poem but not so exacting as to be beyond the
reach of a wide public. In the eighteenth century it was
extremely popular, partly it is true because along with the
Bible and *The Pilgrim's Progress* it was legitimate Sunday
reading for Puritans, but partly because readers of that date
were willing to give steady attention to a few great works.
And it could regain such a vogue whenever a wide public
cared to give it similar attention; the potential attraction,
the perennial human appeal, are there all the time. *Paradise
Regained* is in a different case; it has always been a poem for
the few. But those few have found it, in some strange way,
immensely attractive. Why Milton wrote it we do not
know. The old idea that it is a sequel to *Paradise Lost* does
not work, because the earlier poem had included the

recovery of Paradise through Christ in its scope and had taken world history far beyond the period of time to which *Paradise Regained* is confined. What is certain is that *Paradise Regained* deals once again with the dominant Miltonic theme of the prime importance of the state of mind and the dependence of action on that state.

Paradise Regained is a narrative version of Christ's temptation by the Devil in the wilderness; and in choosing this episode as the chief one in the Gospels Milton was following an earlier tradition particularly dear to Puritan thought. Puritanism loved to picture the Christian life and the chief events leading up to it as a battle. The Christian was a warrior, clad in the spiritual armour listed by St Paul; and there had been two principal battles that had decided his fate. First, the Devil had fought with and defeated Adam, the Old Man, in the Garden of Eden; and secondly, Christ, the New Man, had fought with and defeated the Devil in the wilderness. And the wilderness was necessary for the proper correspondence. As Adam had lost a garden for a wilderness so must Christ conduct his battle in a wilderness to win back the paradisiac garden. Now Milton accepted this rather surprising preference of the Temptation to the Crucifixion partly because he liked to work in the tradition of the religious party to which generally he belonged and partly because the Temptation was in his view the episode which marked the formation of the state of mind which governed all Christ's subsequent action, the acceptance of crucifixion included. Once Christ had acquired that state of mind he had only to act in accordance with it, and action would take care of itself; or rather God in heaven would take care of it. And Christ's victory in the wilderness symbolized the general moral truth that the state of mind comes first and results are subordinate.

Milton's heart was therefore thoroughly in his theme, and in his treatment of it he seems to have consulted his own inclination rather than his readers' applause, in a way different from *Paradise Lost*. There are long speeches and few

deeds. The poem is more of a debate than a narrative; and it
is likely that the Book of Job was Milton's model here. The
language is less ornate and more restricted to simple words
than that of *Paradise Lost*, and the rhythm more subdued
and closer to quiet conversation. This is the cool, quiet,
and yet passionately concentrated way Milton ends the first
book. Satan has just asked with assumed humility permission
to come and talk with Christ in the wilderness:

> To whom our Saviour with unalterd brow.
> Thy coming hither, though I know thy scope,
> I bid not or forbid; do as thou find'st
> Permission from above; thou canst not more.
>   He added not; and Satan bowing low
> His gray dissimulation, disappeard
> Into thin Air diffus'd: for now began
> Night with her sullen wing to double-shade
> The Desert, Fowls in thir clay nests were couch't;
> And now wild Beasts came forth the woods to roam.
>
> (I. 493–502)

It is those already familiar with Milton who will appreciate
this kind of writing. For them the leanness of Christ's
speech will not indicate starvation or poverty but the leanness of the perfectly trained athlete whose body is free from
every trace of superfluous fat and consists of operant bone
and muscle. It will further resemble the athlete's body
when in gentle not in violent motion, gentle but containing
the promise of the fiercest violence, should violence be
required. It is also those already familiar with Milton who
will appreciate the delicate conversational cadence of many
of the speeches. This is Christ speaking of worldly glory:

> But why should man seek glory? who of his own
> Hath nothing, and to whom nothing belongs
> But condemnation, ignominy, and shame?
> Who for so many benefits receiv'd
> Turnd recreant to God, ingrate and false,
> And so of all true good himself despoil'd,
> Yet, sacrilegious to himself would take
> That which to God alone of right belongs;

> Yet so much bounty is in God, such grace,
> That who advance his glory, not thir own,
> Then he himself to glory will advance.   (III. 134-44)

There is no unusual word here, no simile, scarcely a meta-
phor. The effect depends on the verse, the rise and fall of
emphasis within narrow limits, the occasional flicker up of
feeling as in the word 'sacrilegious' as if the poet were
addressing an intimate reader, one who could catch much
meaning from mere hints, one who could take so very
much for granted.

If the conversations are quiet and delicately cadenced, the
landscape is of twilight and suggests less a real scene than a
symbol of the mind's working. But into this dimness
Milton projects brilliant visions which whether by accident
or design resemble the infernal creations which in medieval
romance tempted Sir Galahad in his quest for the Holy
Grail. Here is the description of the phantoms that attended
the banquet Satan raised in the wilderness.

> And at a stately side-board by the wine
> That fragrant smell diffus'd, in order stood
> Tall stripling youths rich clad, of fairer hew
> Then *Ganymed* or *Hylas*; distant more
> Under the Trees now tripd, now solemn stood
> Nymphs of *Diana's* train, and *Naiades*
> With fruits and flowers from *Amalthea's* horn,
> And Ladies of th'*Hesperides*, that seem'd
> Fairer then feignd of old, or fabl'd since
> Of Fairy Damsels met in Forest wide
> By Knights of *Logres*, or of *Lyones*,
> *Lancelot* or *Pelleas*, or *Pellenore*;
> And all the while Harmonious Airs were heard
> Of chiming strings, or charming pipes and winds
> Of gentlest gale *Arabian* odors fannd
> From their soft wings, and *Flora's* earliest smells.
>   (II. 350-65)

Paradise Regained is indeed unusually compounded of twilight, trancelike descriptions, conversations remote from the

market-place or senate-house or inn yet suggesting delicately the cadences of real talk, and brilliant visions. It is a varied and startling composition, but it is strange too; and it is not surprising that in general readers have not been able to take *Paradise Regained* to their hearts.

The case is very different with the other poem published along with *Paradise Regained* in 1674, 'Samson Agonistes'. Milton's Samson, blind and in Philistine captivity, is, like Chaucer's Wife of Bath or Shakespeare's Macbeth or Dickens's Mrs Gamp, one of those figures that help to compose what can be called a nation's literary mythology. Anthony Trollope in his last Barchester novel makes Mr Crawley, himself a tragic figure, talk of Milton's Samson as if he were an accepted national inheritance, the common property of all intelligent readers. Mr Crawley has been making his daughter read about the blinded Polyphemus in the *Odyssey* and he stops her and comments:

The same story is always coming up; we have it in various versions, because it is so true to life.

Ask for this great deliverer now, and find him
Eyeless in Gaza, at the mill with slaves.

It is the same story. Great power reduced to impotence, great glory to misery, by the hand of Fate. At the mill with slaves! Can any picture be more dreadful than that? The mind of the strong blind creature must be so sensible of the injury that has been done to him! The impotency, combined with his strength, or rather the impotency with the memory of former strength and former aspirations, is so essentially tragic.

Aldous Huxley chose *Eyeless in Gaza* for the title of one of his novels. And T. S. Eliot assumed a response he could not assume if he had referred to *Paradise Regained* when he wove references to 'Samson Agontistes' into the texture of 'East Coker':

O dark dark dark. They all go into the dark,
The vacant interstellar spaces, the vacant into the vacant.

Trollope's Mr Crawley was right. Milton's Samson is a terrible yet compelling figure of human suffering, reminding one of Sophocles's Philoctetes, Shakespeare's Lear, and one or two of Hopkins's most poignant sonnets. Milton is surely thinking of the physical pangs of Philoctetes when he makes his Samson burst out into this lyrical complaint:

> O that torment should not be confin'd
> To the bodies wounds and sores
> With maladies innumerable
> In heart, head, brest, and reins;
> But must secret passage find
> To th'inmost mind,
> There exercise all his fierce accidents,
> And on her purest spirits prey,
> As on entrails, joints, and limbs,
> With answerable pains, but more intense,
> Though void of corporal sense.
>   My griefs not only pain me
> As a lingring disease,
> But finding no redress, ferment and rage,
> Nor less then wounds immedicable
> Ranckle, and fester, and gangrene,
> To black mortification.
> Thoughts my Tormentors arm'd with deadly stings
> Mangle my apprehensive tenderest parts,
> Exasperate, exulcerate, and raise
> Dire inflammation which no cooling herb
> Or medcinal liquor can assuage,
> Nor breath of Vernal Air from snowy *Alp*.
> Sleep hath forsook and giv'n me o're
> To deaths benumming Opium as my only cure.
> Thence faintings, swounings of despair,
> And sense of Heav'ns desertion.   (606–32)

But, if Samson the sufferer is a part of English literary mythology, what of the whole play? Here the answer is in some doubt. Milton cannot have written the play to be acted; Samuel Johnson accused it of defective action; and a general notion has prevailed that as a whole it is insufficiently dramatic. And yet 'Samson Agonistes' has been played in amateur performances with great success. The general

notion and the specific event do not concur. The truth is
that Samson is indeed dramatic but in a way unusual in
English drama. There is little action on the stage, the most
important being reported. But there is sufficient action in
Samson's mind. Even so that action is unusual. Motives
on the stage are usually more obvious than they would be in
life. But mental action in Samson does not consist in
obvious changes and transitions but in the spread of an
unconscious temper into consciousness. At the beginning of
the play Samson is in the same case as Adam is in Book X
of *Paradise Lost* when he is in despair and thinks God
has quite cast him off. Actually both Adam and Samson
have accepted complete responsibility for what they have
done and thereby have touched the humility that means
salvation. 'Samson Agonistes' reveals the mind of its pro-
tagonist in its various stages of testing, awakening, compre-
hension, and finds its end in the death of a forgiven and
redeemed hero. As a psychological drama it is a wonderful
and satisfying piece of work. And now that the technique
of choric speech has been improved (mainly through pro-
ductions of T. S. Eliot's verse drama) there is no reason why
'Samson Agonistes' should not take its place as one of the
great acted English classics.

I have written of 'Samson Agonistes' after *Paradise
Regained* as if the facts of simultaneous publication and the
sequence within that publication indicated the same order
of composition. But as already stated there is no certain
proof when 'Samson' was written. Nevertheless it does
supplement *Paradise Regained* very remarkably; and even
if Milton wrote 'Samson' earlier, he may have recast it for
publication. Anyhow if he chose to publish the two poems
together, we are safer in considering them together than in
plumping for earlier dates of composition for which there is
no scrap of firm evidence. Like *Paradise Regained*, 'Samson
Agonistes' deals with the regions of reflection and action.
Christ rejected all temptations to achieve quick results. He
knew his own powers and wondered whether he should

lead Israel to revolt against Rome. But he knew too that such was not his true fate. And he waited till in the fullness of time he achieved a state of mind that insured that all his actions would be soundly based. Samson on the other hand chose a life of physical action and up to a point he was right, because he had been gifted with unusual strength. But success corrupted him and made him overvalue his gift. Through this pride he fell into misfortune, but he recognized his error and fell into the extremes of despair and humility:

> O impotence of mind, in body strong!
> But what is strength without a double share
> Of wisdom, vast, unwieldy, burdensom,
> Proudly secure, yet liable to fall
> By weakest suttleties, not made to rule,
> But to subserve where wisdom bears command.   (52–7)

Once Samson has realized that the state of mind comes first, once his own state of mind is sound, God allows him yet again to put his gift of unusual physical strength into action. The idea of the two poems is the same; but in the first the climax is the achievement of a state of mind implying perfect actions to come, in the second a piece of action based on a sound state of mind already achieved.

I think myself that *Paradise Lost* is worth more than all the rest of Milton's works put together, but it is true that fewer readers than in former times have the patience to master a long poem. The almost superstitious reverence for the successful epic has disappeared. It may be that for some years to come the early poems, fragments of *Paradise Lost*, 'Samson Agonistes' and perhaps *Areopagitica* will be the *operant* portions of his works. It is to be regretted if this should be so, but even if thus truncated Milton survives as a major poet of surpassing power and variety.

MILTON
A Select Bibliography
(Place of publication London, unless stated otherwise)

Bibliography:

A CONCORDANCE TO THE POETICAL WORKS OF JOHN MILTON, ed.
J. Bradshaw (1894)
—reprinted 1965.

FACSIMILE OF THE MANUSCRIPT OF MILTON'S MINOR POEMS PRESERVED
IN THE LIBRARY OF TRINITY COLLEGE, CAMBRIDGE, published by
W. A. Wright; Cambridge (1899)
—reproduced in part by F. A. Patterson, Facsimile Text Society,
New York, 1933; Scolar Press facsimile, Menston, 1970.

LEXICON TO THE ENGLISH POETICAL WORKS OF JOHN MILTON, by L. E.
Lockwood; New York (1907).

MILTON, 1608-1674: Facsimile of the Autographs and Documents in
the British Museum (1908).

JOHN MILTON: A Topical Bibliography, by E. N. S. Thompson;
New Haven (1916).

A GEOGRAPHICAL DICTIONARY OF MILTON, by A. H. Gilbert; New
Haven (1919).

A CONCORDANCE OF THE LATIN, GREEK AND ITALIAN POEMS OF JOHN
MILTON, ed. L. Cooper; Halle (1923).

A MILTON HANDBOOK, by J. H. Hanford; New York (1926)
—fifth revised edition, 1970.

REFERENCE GUIDE TO MILTON FROM 1800 TO THE PRESENT DAY, by
D. H. Stevens; Chicago (1930).

CONTRIBUTIONS TO A MILTON BIBLIOGRAPHY, 1800-1930: Being a List
of Addenda to Stevens's Reference Guide, ed. H. F. Fletcher;
Urbana (1931).

THE ENGLISH RENAISSANCE 1510-1688, by V. de S. Pinto (1938)
—third revised edition, 1966. Contains a bibliography.

JOHN MILTON: A Bibliographical Supplement, 1929-1957, by
C. Huckabay; Pittsburgh & Louvain (1960)
—revised ed., 1969, under the title *John Milton: An annotated
bibliography, 1929-1968.*

A MILTON DICTIONARY, by E. S. Le Comte; New York (1960)
—English edition, 1961.

A CONCORDANCE TO MILTON'S ENGLISH POETRY, ed. W. Ingram and
K. Swaim; Oxford (1972).

Collected Works:

A COMPLETE COLLECTION OF THE HISTORICAL, POLITICAL, AND MISCEL-
LANEOUS WORKS OF MILTON, ed. J. Toland, 3 vols (1694-8).

POETICAL WORKS, together with Explanatory Notes on Each Book of
the *Paradise Lost*, and a Table never before printed, ed. P[atrick]
H[ume], 5 parts (1695)
—the first collected edition of the poetry.

POETICAL WORKS. With the Principal Notes of Various Commentators,
ed. H. J. Todd (6 vols, 1801; 7 vols, 1809, with additions and a
verbal index)
—a variorum edition using the work of some of the best-known
eighteenth-century editors of Milton including R. Bentley,
T. Newton, and Thomas Warton. This edition also contains critical
appreciation of Milton by Andrew Marvell, Dryden, Addison,
Thomson, Dr Johnson, Gray, Cowper, etc.

COWPER'S MILTON, with Notes by William Cowper, ed. W. Hayley,
4 vols; Chichester (1810).

PROSE WORKS, ed. J. A. St John, 5 vols (1848-53).

WORKS, IN VERSE AND PROSE, ed. J. Mitford, 8 vols (1851)
—complete except for 'Of Christian Doctrine' and minor items.

ENGLISH POEMS, ed. R. C. Browne (1866)
—with notes by H. Bradley, 1894.

POETICAL WORKS, ed. D. Masson, 3 vols (1874)
—revised edition, 1890. The Globe, one-vol ed., with introduction
by D. Masson, was published in 1877.

THE CAMBRIDGE MILTON FOR SCHOOLS, ed. A. W. Verity, 11 vols
(1891-9).

THE POETICAL WORKS OF JOHN MILTON, ed. H. C. Beeching; Oxford
(1900)
—revised edition, 1938.

POETICAL WORKS, ed. W. Aldis Wright (1903)
—the best modernized text.

THE POEMS OF JOHN MILTON, arranged in Chronological Order, ed.
H. J. C. Grierson, 2 vols (1925).

THE STUDENT'S MILTON, ed. F. A. Patterson; New York (1930)
—contains the complete poetry and most of the prose in one volume.
Early biographies of Milton are included. Revised edition in 1933,

with annotations to the poetry and prose. An indispensable edition for the student.

WORKS, edited by various hands under the general editorship of F. A. Patterson; New York (1931-8)
—this Columbia University Edition in 18 volumes is the only complete edition of Milton's works. The last volume contains previously uncollected writings and marginalia. There is a two-volume index edited by F. A. Patterson and F. R. Fogle, which forms an invaluable work of reference, New York, 1940.

PRIVATE CORRESPONDENCE AND ACADEMIC EXERCISES, translated from the Latin by P. B. Tillyard, with an introduction and commentary by E. M. W. Tillyard; Cambridge (1932).

THE POEMS OF JOHN MILTON, ed. J. H. Hanford; New York (1936).

COMPLETE POETRY AND SELECTED PROSE, ed. E. H. Visiak (1938).

COMPLETE POETICAL WORKS, a new text edition with introduction and notes, ed. H. F. Fletcher; Boston (1941)
—a revision of the Cambridge edition, edited by W. V. Moody.

COMPLETE POETICAL WORKS, reproduced in photographic facsimile, ed. H. F. Fletcher, 4 vols; Urbana (1943-8).

JOHN MILTON, COMPLETE POEMS AND MAJOR PROSE, edited with notes by M. Y. Hughes; New York (1957).

POETICAL WORKS, ed. H. Darbishire (1958)
—in the Oxford Standard Authors edition.

THE COMPLETE PROSE WORKS, ed. D. M. Wolfe and others, 5 vols; Yale, New Haven (1953-70).

COMPLETE POETICAL WORKS, ed. D. Bush; Boston (1965)
—English edition, 1966.

THE POEMS OF JOHN MILTON, ed. J. Carey and A. Fowler (1968).

Selected Works:

POEMS OF MR JOHN MILTON. Both English and Latin. Compos'd at several times. Printed . . . for H. Moseley (1645)
—the Minor Poems, including 'On the Morning of Christ's Nativity', 'L'Allegro', 'Il Penseroso', Sonnets and other poems. Facsimile reprint of the English poems, 1968.

POEMS, ETC. UPON SEVERAL OCCASIONS. By Mr John Milton: Both English and Latin, etc., composed at several times. With a small Tractate of Education to Mr Hartlib (1673).

LATIN AND ITALIAN POEMS OF MILTON, translated by William Cowper, ed. W. Hayley, Chichester, 1808; *Latin Poems* ed. with translation by W. MacKellar, New Haven, 1930.

[MINOR POEMS], ed. O. Elton, 5 vols; Oxford (1893-1900).

SONNETS, with original notes and new biographical matter, ed. J. S. Smart; Glasgow (1921).

THE PORTABLE MILTON, ed. with an introduction by D. Bush; New York (1949).

POEMS OF MR JOHN MILTON, the 1645 edition, with essays in analysis by C. Brooks and J. E. Hardy; New York (1951)
—reissued, London, 1957.

Separate Works:

AN EPITAPH ON THE ADMIRABLE DRAMATICKE POET, W. SHAKESPEARE
—first published in the Second Folio of Shakespeare's Plays (1632).

A MASKE PRESENTED AT LUDLOW CASTLE, 1634. On Michaelmasse night, before the Right Honourable, John Earle of Bridgewater (1637)
—the title *Comus* was first used in the stage version of 1738.

LYCIDAS (1638)
—in a collection of memorial verses, Latin, Greek, and English, entitled *Obsequies To The Memory Of Mr Edward King.*

EPITAPHIUM DAMONIS [DAMON'S EPITAPH] (1640?)
—unique copy in the British Museum.

OF REFORMATION TOUCHING CHURCH-DISCIPLINE IN ENGLAND: and the Causes that hitherto have hindred it; Two books, written to a Freind (1641).

OF PRELATICAL EPISCOPACY, and Whither it may be deduc'd from the Apostolical times by vertue of those Testimonies which are alledg'd to that purpose in some late Treatises: One whereof goes under the Name of James Archbishop of Armagh (1641).

ANIMADVERSIONS UPON THE REMONSTRANTS DEFENCE AGAINST SMECTYMNUUS (1641).

THE REASON OF CHURCH-GOVERNMENT URG'D AGAINST PRELATY. In two Books (1641).

AN APOLOGY AGAINST A PAMPHLET call'd A modest Confutation of the Animadversions upon the Remonstrant against Smectymnuus (1642).

THE DOCTRINE AND DISCIPLINE OF DIVORCE: restor'd to the good of both sexes, From the bondage of Canon Law; and other mistakes, to Christian freedom, guided by the Rule of Charity (1643)
—second edition, revised and augmented, 1644.

OF EDUCATION. To Master Samuel Hartlib [1644].

THE JUDGEMENT OF MARTIN BUCER, concerning Divorce. Writt'n to Edward the sixt, in his second Book of the Kingdom of Christ, And now Englisht (1644).

AREOPAGITICA: a Speech of Mr John Milton for the Liberty of Unlicenc'd Printing, to the Parliament of England (1644).

TETRACHORDON: Expositions Upon the foure chief places in Scripture which treat of Mariage, or nullities in Mariage (1645).

COLASTERION: A Reply to A Nameles Answer against The Doctrine and Discipline of Divorce (1645).

[SONNET TO HENRY LAWES]. In *Choice Psalms, Put Into Music For Three Voices*. Compos'd by Henry and William Lawes (1648).

THE TENURE OF KINGS AND MAGISTRATES (1649).

OBSERVATIONS UPON THE ARTICLES OF PEACE WITH THE IRISH REBELS, on the letter of Ormond to Col. Jones, and the Representation of the Presbytery at Belfast (1649).

ΕΙΚΟΝΟΚΛΑΣΤΗΣ [EIKONOKLASTES]: In Answer to a Book Intitl'd *Εἰκὼν Βασιλική* [Eikon Basilike], The Portrature of his Sacred Majesty in his Solitudes and Sufferings (1649)
—second edition, much enlarged, 1650.

PRO POPULO ANGLICANO DEFENSIO, contra Claudii Anonymi, alias Salmasii Defensionem regiam [A DEFENCE OF THE PEOPLE OF ENGLAND . . . in answer to Salmasius's defence of the King] (1651)
—translated by J. Washington, 1692.

A LETTER WRITTEN TO A GENTLEMAN IN THE COUNTRY, touching the Dissolution of the late Parliament and the Reasons thereof (1653).

PRO POPULO ANGLICANO DEFENSIO SECUNDA, contra infamem libellum anonymum cui titulus, Regii sanguinis clamor ad coelum adversus parricidas Anglicanos [SECOND DEFENCE OF THE PEOPLE OF ENGLAND] (1654)
—translated by F. Wrangham, 1816.

JOANNIS MILTONII PRO SE DEFENSIO, contra Alexandrum Morum Ecclesiasten Libelli famosi, cui titulus, Regii sanguinis clamor ad coelum adversus parricidas Anglicanos, authorem recte dictum [JOHN MILTON'S DEFENCE FOR HIMSELF] (1655).

A TREATISE OF CIVIL POWER IN ECCLESIASTICAL CAUSES, shewing that it is not lawfull for any power on earth to compell in matters of religion (1659).

CONSIDERATIONS TOUCHING THE LIKELIEST MEANS TO REMOVE HIRELINGS OUT OF THE CHURCH (1659).

BRIEF NOTES UPON A LATE SERMON, Titl'd, The Fear of God and the King; Preach'd, and since Publish'd, by Matthew Griffith, DD, and Chaplain to the late King (1660).

THE READIE & EASIE WAY TO ESTABLISH A FREE COMMONWEALTH, and the Excellence thereof compar'd with the inconveniences and dangers of readmitting kingship in this nation (1660).

PARADISE LOST. A Poem Written in Ten Books. By John Milton (1667) —published in Twelve Books in The Second Edition, Revised and Augmented, 1674. A Facsimile reproduction of the First Edition with an introduction by D. Masson was published in 1877. The Manuscript of Book I was edited by H. Darbishire, Oxford, 1931.

THE HISTORY OF BRITAIN, That Part especially now call'd England (1670).

PARADISE REGAIN'D: A Poem in IV Books. To which is added 'Samson Agonistes' (1671).

OF TRUE RELIGION, HÆRESIE, SCHISM, TOLERATION, and what best means may be us'd against the growth of Popery (1673).

MR JOHN MILTON'S CHARACTER OF THE LONG PARLIAMENT AND ASSEMBLY OF DIVINES. In MDCXLI. Omitted in his Works, and never before Printed, and very seasonable for these times (1681) —originally part of Book III of The History of Britain.

A BRIEF HISTORY OF MOSCOVIA, and other less known Countries lying eastward of Russia as far as Cathay (1682).

LETTERS OF STATE, Written by Mr John Milton . . . From the year 1649 Till 1659. To Which is added, An Account of his Life (by E. Phillips). Together with several of his Poems; and a Catalogue of his Works, never before Printed (1694).

DE DOCTRINA CHRISTIANA, libri duo posthumi [A TREATISE OF CHRISTIAN DOCTRINE], compiled from the Holy Scriptures alone, ed. C. R. Sumner; Cambridge (1825)
—translated by C. R. Sumner, Cambridge, 1825.

Some Biographical and Critical Studies:

Note: Early biographies of Milton by John Aubrey, Anthony Wood, Edward Phillips, John Toland, Jonathan Richardson, and Thomas Ellwood, are collected in *The Student's Milton* (1930). See also *Early Lives of Milton*, by H. Darbishire (1932).

ON PARADISE LOST, by A. Marvell (1674)
—a poem in praise of Milton, prefixed to the 1674 edition of *Paradise Lost*.

APOLOGY FOR HEROIC POETRY, by J. Dryden (1677)
—printed in *Essays*, Selected and edited by W. P. Ker, Oxford, 1900.

[PAPERS ON PARADISE LOST], by J. Addison (1711-12)
—published in the *Spectator* from 31 December 1711 to 3 May 1712 (No 267 and on Saturdays until No 369). Twelve papers discuss the beauties of each of the twelve books. Six papers discuss *Paradise Lost* as a whole.

EXPLANATORY NOTES AND REMARKS ON MILTON'S PARADISE LOST, by J. Richardson (1734).

AN ESSAY ON THE GENIUS AND WRITINGS OF POPE, by J. Warton (1756)
—an interesting eighteenth-century estimate of Milton in relation to Pope.

LIFE OF MILTON, by S. Johnson (1779)
—published in his *Lives of the English Poets*.

IMAGINARY CONVERSATIONS, by W. S. Landor (1824-9)
—contains two 'conversations' between Milton and Marvell, ed. C. G. Crump, 1891.

LITERARY REMAINS, by S. T. Coleridge, ed. H. N. Coleridge (1836-9)
—contains a lecture on Milton delivered in 1818. See also Coleridge's comparison of Milton and Shakespeare in *Biographia Literaria*, ch. xv, 1817.

THE LIFE OF JOHN MILTON: Narrated in Connexion with the Political, Ecclesiastical, and Literary History of His Time, by D. Masson, 7 vols (1858-81)
—with index, 1894.

CRITICAL AND HISTORICAL ESSAYS, CONTRIBUTED TO THE EDINBURGH REVIEW, 3 vols, by T. B. Macaulay (1843)
—contains the famous essay on Milton published in August, 1825. See also *Miscellaneous Writings*, 1860.

MIXED ESSAYS, by M. Arnold (1879)
—see also his *Essays in Criticism, Second Series*, 1888.

LITERARY STUDIES, by W. Bagehot, ed. R. H. Hutton (1879)
—contains a study of Milton.

MILTON, by M. Pattison (1879)
—in the 'English Men of Letters' series.

LIFE OF JOHN MILTON, by R. Garnett (1890).

MILTON'S PROSODY, by R. Bridges; Oxford (1893)
—a revised version of two essays, 1887 and 1889; revised ed., 1901; another edition with a chapter on accentual verse, and notes, 1921.

MILTON, by Sir W. A. Raleigh (1900).

THE CLASSICAL MYTHOLOGY OF MILTON'S ENGLISH POEMS, by C. G. Osgood; New Haven (1900)
—Yale Studies in English, No. 8; reprinted, Oxford, 1925.

THE EPIC, by L. Abercrombie (1914)
—contains important criticism of Milton's epics.

THE INFLUENCE OF MILTON ON ENGLISH POETRY, by R. D. Havens; Cambridge, Mass. (1922).

MILTON: Man and Thinker, by D. Saurat; New York (1925)
—a translation and adaptation of essays earlier published in French. Contains a bibliography of criticism of Milton.

A MILTON HANDBOOK, by J. H. Hanford; New York (1926)
—fifth revised edition, 1970. See also this author's *The Youth of Milton* in Univ. of Michigan *Studies of Shakespeare, Milton, and Donne*, New York, 1925.

CROSS CURRENTS IN ENGLISH LITERATURE OF THE XVIITH CENTURY, by H. J. C. Grierson (1929)
—the Messenger lectures, Cornell University, 1926-7.

POETS AND PLAYWRIGHTS: Shakespeare, Jonson, Spenser, Milton, by E. E. Stoll; Minneapolis (1930).

MILTON, by E. M. W. Tillyard (1930)
—a full treatment of Milton's literary and mental development.
Revised ed., 1966.

SELECTED ESSAYS, 1917-1932, by T. S. Eliot (1932)
—T. S. Eliot's observations on Milton which appeared in this volume
were later amplified in his lecture on Milton in the British Academy
'Annual Lecture on a Master Mind', 1947.

MILTON, by R. Macaulay (1934)
—revised ed., 1957.

REVALUATION, by F. R. Leavis (1936)
—contains important essay on Milton. See also *The Common Pursuit*,
1952.

MILTON AND WORDSWORTH, POETS AND PROPHETS: A Study of their
Reactions to Political Events, by H. J. C. Grierson; Cambridge
(1937).

THE MILTONIC SETTING, PAST AND PRESENT, by E. M. W. Tillyard;
Cambridge (1938)
—a study of Milton's seventeenth-century setting and his present
poetic status.

MILTON ON HIMSELF: Milton's utterances upon himself and his work,
ed. J. S. Diekhoff (1939)
—new ed., 1965.

THIS GREAT ARGUMENT: A Study of Milton's *De Doctrina Christiana*
as a gloss upon *Paradise Lost*, by M. Kelley; Princeton (1941).

MILTON IN THE PURITAN REVOLUTION, by D. Wolfe; New York (1941)
—study of the political significance of Milton's work.

A PREFACE TO PARADISE LOST, by C. S. Lewis (1942)
—a study of the poem's Christian background.

PARADISE LOST IN OUR TIME: SOME COMMENTS, by D. Bush; Ithaca,
N.Y. (1945)
—a defence of Milton against his modern detractors.

PROPHETS OF HEAVEN AND HELL: Virgil, Dante, Milton, Goethe: an
Introductory Essay, by C. R. Buxton; Cambridge (1945).

MILTON'S PARADISE LOST: A Commentary on the Argument, by
J. S. Diekhoff; New York (1946).

PARADISE LOST AND THE SEVENTEENTH CENTURY READER, by B. Rajan
(1947).

PARADISE LOST AND ITS CRITICS, by A. J. A. Waldock; Cambridge (1947)
—an able and coolly provocative statement of doubt whether the poem is a consistent whole.

JOHN MILTON, by R. Warner (1949).

THE LIFE RECORDS OF JOHN MILTON, ed. J. M. French, 4 vols; New Brunswick (1949-58).

STUDIES IN MILTON, by E. Tillyard (1951)
—in this book Dr Tillyard aims largely at supplementing and correcting some matters in his *Milton*. A study on the crisis of *Paradise Lost* corrects a common assumption and advances a general interpretation of the Ninth and Tenth Books.

THE ITALIAN ELEMENT IN MILTON'S VERSE, by F. T. Prince; Oxford (1954)
—an original study embodying new discoveries.

THE HARMONIOUS VISION: Studies in Milton's poetry, by D. C. Allen; Baltimore (1954)
—enlarged ed., 1970.

JOHN MILTON, by K. Muir (1955).

THE INTELLECTUAL DEVELOPMENT OF JOHN MILTON, by H. F. Fletcher, 2 vols; Urbana (1956-61).

THE METAPHYSICALS AND MILTON, by E. M. W. Tillyard (1956).

MILTON, by D. Daiches (1957).

IMAGES & THEMES IN FIVE POEMS BY MILTON, by R. Tuve; Cambridge, Mass. (1957).

A CRITIQUE OF PARADISE LOST, by J. Peter (1960)
—an honest and erudite attempt to define what is left of *Paradise Lost* when its many defects are taken into account.

SOME GRAVER SUBJECT: An Essay on *Paradise Lost*, by J. B. Broadbent (1960)
—a penetrating microscopic analysis of the way *Paradise Lost* evolves.

THE LIVING MILTON: Essays by Various Hands, ed. F. Kermode (1960).

MILTON'S GOD, by W. Empson (1961)
—rev. edition with new appendix, 1965.

MILTON: COMUS AND SAMSON AGONISTES, by J. B. Broadbent (1961).

THE MUSE'S METHOD: An Introduction to *Paradise Lost*, by J. H. Summers (1962).

MILTON'S PARADISE LOST, by B. A. Wright (1962).

MILTON'S GRAND STYLE, by C. Ricks; Oxford (1963).

MILTON'S EPIC VOICE: The Narrator in *Paradise Lost*, by A. D. Ferry; Cambridge, Mass. (1963).

DANTE, MICHELANGELO AND MILTON, by J. Arthos (1963).

JOHN MILTON: A sketch of his Life and Writings, by D. Bush; New York (1964).

MILTON CRITICISM: Selections from four centuries, ed. J. Thorpe (1965).

A READING OF PARADISE LOST, by H. Gardner; Oxford (1966)
—the Alexander lectures, University of Toronto, 1962.

TEN PERSPECTIVES OF MILTON, by M. Y. Hughes; New Haven (1965).

MILTON: The Modern Phase. A Study of Twentieth-Century Criticism, by P. Murray (1967).

MILTON AND THE CHRISTIAN TRADITION, by C. A. Patrides; Oxford (1967).

DANTE AND MILTON: The *Commedia* and *Paradise Lost*, by I. Samuel (1967).

MILTON AND THE RENAISSANCE HERO, by J. M. Steadman (1967).

MILTON: A biography, by W. R. Parker, 2 vols; Oxford (1968).

MILTON AND THE ITALIAN CITIES, by J. Arthos (1968).

MILTON AND THE MASQUE TRADITION: The early poems, 'Arcades' and 'Comus', by J. G. Demaray; Cambridge, Mass. & London (1968).

MILTON'S POETIC ART: *A Mask*, *Lycidas* and *Paradise Lost*, by J. Reesing; Harvard (1968).

MILTON, by J. Carey (1969).

CRITICAL ESSAYS ON MILTON FROM E.L.H.; Baltimore (1969)
—reprints articles from the *Journal of English Literary History*, 1935-68.

MILTON'S MINOR POEMS, by J. B. Leishman, ed. G. Tillotson (1969).

MILTON AND HIS WORLD, by C. V. Wedgwood (1969).

MILTON STUDIES, ed. J. D. Simmonds; Pittsburgh (1969-).

MILTON: The Critical Heritage, ed. J. T. Shawcross (1970).

MILTON AND THE IDEA OF MATRIMONY: A Study of the Divorce Tracts and *Paradise Lost*, by J. Halkett; New Haven (1970).

A VARIORUM COMMENTARY ON THE POEMS OF JOHN MILTON (1970-)
—Vol 1: The Latin and Greek poems, by D. Bush; The Italian poems, by J. E. Shaw and A. Bartlett Giamatti, 1970.

THE ROMANTICS ON MILTON: Formal essays and critical asides, ed. J. A. Wittreich; Cleveland (1971).

MILTON'S CREATION: A Guide through *Paradise Lost*, by H. Blamires (1971).

REINTERPRETATIONS: Essays on poems by Milton, Pope and Johnson, by J. P. Hardy (1971).

A PREFACE TO MILTON, by L. Potter (1971).

ARISTOTLE'S THEORY AND MILTON'S PRACTICE: SAMSON AGONISTES, by B. R. Rees; Birmingham (1972).

Miscellaneous:

(1) *Milton's Illustrators:*

William Blake made 53 illustrations for Milton's poetry, including 2 sets of 8 water-colour drawings for *Comus* (1801), 12 water-colour drawings for *Paradise Lost* (1807) and a second set of 9 drawings in 1808, 6 water-colour drawings for the 'Nativity Ode' (1809), 12 designs illustrating 'L'Allegro' and 'Il Penseroso' (about 1816), and 12 water-colour drawings for *Paradise Regained* (about 1816).

See *John Milton, Poems in English with Illustrations by William Blake*, ed. G. Keynes (1926).

Other major illustrators of Milton were Fuseli (1802) and John Martin (1824-6).

(2) *Milton's Poetry set to Music:*

Henry Lawes composed the music for *Comus* in 1634. Milton's 'Sonnet to Henry Lawes' was set to music by Henry and William Lawes and appeared in *Choice Palmes, Put into Musick for Three voices* (1648).

In 1677 Dryden wrote a rhymed opera, *The State of Innocence*, based on *Paradise Lost*.

(3) *The Portraits of Milton:*

MILTON TERCENTENARY: The Portraits, Prints and Writings of John Milton, Exhibited at Christ's College, Cambridge, 1908, by G. C. Williamson; Cambridge (1908).

THE BEVERLEY CHEW COLLECTION OF MILTON PORTRAITS, by R. S. Granniss, New York (1926).

WRITERS AND THEIR WORK

Learning Resources Center
Sampson Technical Institute
Clinton, N. C. 28328